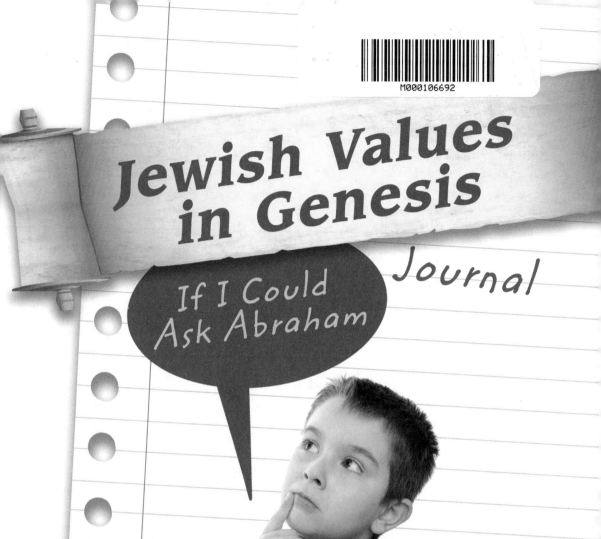

Jewish Values in Genesis

If I Could Ask Abraham

Journal

by Rachael Gelfman Schultz

BEHRMAN HOUSE
www.behrmanhouse.com

To the Educator: Please refer to the accompanying Lesson Plan Manual for complete lesson plans, background information, project ideas, and more. Visit www.behrmanhouse.com/values-bible for further resources.

Designer: Terry Taylor Studio
Project editor: Dena Neusner
Editorial consultants: Ellen Rank, Diane Zimmerman

Copyright © 2015 Behrman House, Inc.
Springfield, New Jersey 07081
www.behrmanhouse.com
Printed in the United States of America

Library of Congress Cataloging-in-Publication Data

Schultz, Rachael Gelfman, author.

Jewish values in Genesis : if I could ask Abraham / by Rachael Gelfman Schultz.

pages cm

"This work consists of two complementary books. The Student Response Journal includes creative, interactive activities, integrating Jewish texts with journal writing, drama, art, music, movement, and more. The Teacher Resource presents 14 ready-to-use lesson plans of approximately 50 minutes each for Jewish values in Genesis: If I Could Ask Abraham. It includes suggestions for teaching every element of the Student Response Journal"--Introduction.

Grades 4-6.

ISBN 978-0-87441-925-2

1. Bible. Genesis--Textbooks for children. 2. Jewish ethics--Biblical teaching--Textbooks for children. 3. Jewish religious education--Activity programs. I. Title.

BS1239.S38 2015

296.6'8083--dc23

2014046367

The publisher gratefully acknowledges the following sources of photographs and graphic images:
(T=top, B=bottom, M=middle, L=left, R=right)

COVER: Shutterstock: Ozgur Coskun (boy), KUCO (scroll sketch), Art'nLera (light bulb, scale, arrows), A-R-T (parchment), Blend Images (girl); Wikimedia Commons/www.bassenge.com (Noah); Fotolia/Fotolial (Torah). INTERIOR: Shutterstock: Veronica Louro 2-3, 39L, Blend Images 4 TL, 4 TR, 5T, Mikhail 4M, Lapina 5ML, Ruslan Guzov 5 MR, Evgeny Atamanenko 6, Ghenadie 7L (Torah icon), solarseven 7R, BThaiMan 8T (shovel icon), Luminis 8B, Nomad_Soul 9T (puzzle icon), Art'nLera 10T (light bulb icon), Gelpi JM 10-11B, Digital Storm 12, SiuWing 13 (timeline icon), Diego Cervo 14B, 18B, wawritto 15B, valdis torms 19T (scale icon), Syda Productions 21M, jorisvo 22M, Monkey Business Images 23, Adisa 27, Aleutie 28BL, Peter Polak 28BR, Goldenarts 29T, Iakov Filimonov 32B, gpointstudio 34, Victor V. Hoguns Zhugin 35R, Glenda 39R, Denizo71 41L, Nolte Lourens 41R, Denis Kuvaev 41R, marekuliasz 43L, Lucky Business 43R, Stuart Miles 44L, racorn 44R, Aquir 47L, Gunnar Pippel 47R, globe 48R, Dragon Images 49L, Frances L. Fruit 49R, Yulia Glam 52TL, alexwhite 52-53 (question mark), Best Choice 52B, All Vectors 53M, tkemot 53B, Hung Chung Chih 54, Suzanne Tucker 55, Anelina 60B, Creativa Images 61T, Gladskikh Tatiana 62, MJTH 64, clearviewstock 66B, Africa Studio 67R, Olesia Bilkei 68; Wikimedia Commons: 14T, 19M, 20T, 30B, 37B, 50, 69TR, 69M, 69B, Titimaster 9B, Michel Wolgemut and Wilhelm Pleydenwurff 15R, www.bassenge.com 17R, Suwan Wanawattanawong 17R, Provident Lithograph Company 4B, 20B, 40, Csanady 24B, Google Cultural Institute 26B, Bridgeman Art Library 31T, The Yorck Project 37TR, GFreihalter 37B, Web Gallery of Art 45R, 46, 58, www.oldbookart.com 56T, 56B, 57T, 57B, www.abcgallery.com 65, National Library of Israel 70TL; Other sources: GoodSalt Inc/ Standard Publishing 19B; JWA/ Sally J. Preisand 20M; Terry Taylor 25, 61B; Risa Towbin Aqua 30M; Israeli Government Press Office/Israeli Tsvika 31M; bibleinpictures.com 51; Yad Vashem 70M.

CONTENTS

Introduction

What do the people in the Bible have to do with me and my family?

What can the Torah have to say about how I lead my life today?

The Torah is the story of our people.

It is a story that Jews have told **again and again** from Biblical times until today. Why do we keep telling this story from one generation to the next? Each time that we tell the story, we learn something new about ourselves and our relationships. We learn important Jewish values that continue to guide us **today**.

Our biblical ancestors lived in a world very different from ours, but

they had many of the same challenges and successes in their relationships that we do. Sometimes we will learn from what the people in the Bible **did right**; other times we will learn from their **mistakes**.

In this book, we will look at Jewish values that we learn from stories in **Genesis,** the first book of the Torah. Each chapter will focus primarily on one Jewish value or *midah* (מִדָּה — positive character trait) and one key story from Genesis. In the first three chapters, we will use these stories to look inward and explore the **self**—who am I and what is important to me? In chapters four through seven, we will look at our **relationships** with those closest to us, our families.

We will meet many interesting **people from the Bible** and from Jewish history, and we will see how their choices demonstrate (or don't demonstrate) the values that we are studying. As we learn about these people, your job is to **ask questions** about them and how they lived their lives. What Jewish values helped them make good choices? What was hard for them and why? You will choose one of these people to learn more about and do a creative project to share what you've learned.

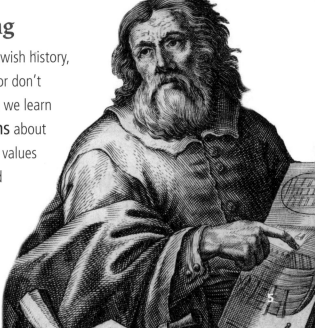

Who Am I?
Creation

Essential Questions: We learn from the story of the Creation of the world that all people are created in the image of God. What does this mean for how we treat others and ourselves? What makes each of us unique?

Get on the Move

Walk around the room quietly. Then walk around the room as if you are…

- A toddler who has just learned to walk
- A class bully
- President of the United States
- Created from dust
- Created in God's image (in some way like God)

(Don't stop to think about these phrases right now, and don't worry if you don't understand them fully. Just walk in the first way that comes to mind for each of them.)

How did you walk when you imagined you were created from dust?

_____

_____

_____

How did you walk when you imagined you were created in God's image?

_____

_____

_____

Creation

In the book of Genesis, chapter 1, the Torah describes the Creation of the world in six days. People are created last, on the sixth day of Creation. We read:

> God created man in God's own image, in the image of God [b'tzelem Elohim]…male and female, God created them. And God blessed them, and God said to them: "Be fruitful and multiply; fill the earth and master it; rule over the fish of the sea, and the birds of the air, and over every living thing that crawls on the earth." (Genesis 1:27–28)

In chapter 2 of Genesis, we read a very different description of the creation of people:

> God formed a person from the dust of the ground and breathed into his nostrils the breath of life, and he became a living soul….God took the person and put him in the Garden of Eden to work it and care for it.
> (Genesis 2:7,15)

Fill in the chart comparing and contrasting these two different descriptions of God creating people:

	Chapter 1	Chapter 2
How were people created?		
What are they supposed to do in the world?		
What words would you use to describe people based on this Creation story?		

Which description of the creation of people do you like better? Why?

_____

_____

Why do you think the Torah gives us two different descriptions of how people were created?

_____

_____

Digging Deeper

We learn from the Torah that each person is created in the image of God; each of us is like God in some important ways. Whatever your personal beliefs are, the Creation story can help us think about what it means to be human and how we can each be our best possible selves.

In what ways can a person be like God? What traits does God have that we can have too?

_____

_____

_____

What can we learn about ourselves from the Torah's statement that we are all created in the image of God? (Remember how you walked when you imagined yourself created in the image of God.)

_____

_____

_____

I have these questions about God: _____

_____

_____

_____

_____

_____

_____

Making Meaning
בְּצֶלֶם אֱ-לֹהִים

B'tzelem Elohim is a Hebrew phrase that means "in the image of God."

When the Torah tells us that we are all created in God's image, what can we learn from this about how to live our lives? How can you treat yourself and others in keeping with this idea? Make a list.

I can… (check all that apply)

☐ Invite the new kid in my class over to my home.

☐ Volunteer at a soup kitchen.

☐ Walk to school instead of driving.

☐ _____

☐ _____

☐ _____

☐ _____

☐ _____

☐ _____

☐ _____

Creation of Adam, detail from the Sistine Chapel, Michelangelo

Try This!

Seeing each person as being created in God's image means seeing the good in each person.

Sit in a circle with your classmates. Go around the room taking turns telling the person next to you one positive thing that makes that person unique. Try to think of something that comes from inside that person, rather than focusing on appearances or possessions.

Rabbis' Corner

The ancient rabbis teach:

> The first person was created alone in order to…tell of the greatness of the Holy Blessed One. For if a person makes many coins from one mold, all the coins are exactly alike. But though the…Holy Blessed One made every person from the mold of the first person, not a single one of them is exactly alike. (Babylonian Talmud, *Sanhedrin* 37a)

What are the pros and cons of each person being unique and not exactly like another?

Pros	Cons

What Makes Me Unique?

Make a collage or a drawing showing what makes you who you are. What are some of the unique things about you that people don't always see?

The One and Only

Being unique also means that each person has something special to contribute to the world. What are some of the ways that only you can help those around you—your family, friends, classmates, and others—and make their lives a little better?

Only I can _____

_____

_____

_____

_____

I can also _____

_____

_____

_____

_____

I will try my best to _____

_____

_____

_____

Torah Timeline:
Why Do We Want What We Can't Have?

Creation of World   **Adam and Eve**   **Cain and Abel**   **Noah and the Flood**

Through the Creation story, we learn that each person has unique blessings—qualities and talents that make him or her special. Yet this means that other people have blessings that we don't have or that we may want for ourselves. The Torah tells two stories about what happens when people want what they can't have.

In the first story, Adam and Eve live in the Garden of Eden, where all of their needs are met, and they do not have to work for their food. God commands them: "You may eat freely of all the trees of the Garden [of Eden], but you may not eat from the tree of knowledge of good and evil...."
(Genesis 2:16–17) The snake, however, tempts Eve, and she eats from the tree, as does Adam. In response, God sends them away from the Garden of Eden, and they are forced to work to bring food from the land.

In the second story (Genesis 4:1–16), Eve gives birth to Cain and then Abel. Cain grows up and becomes a farmer, while Abel becomes a shepherd. One day, Cain brings God a sacrifice of the fruits of the land, and Abel brings God a sacrifice of the best of his sheep. God accepts Abel's offering but not Cain's offering. Cain becomes very angry and kills his brother.

Talk about It:

- Why do you think Adam and Eve choose to eat fruit from the one tree that is forbidden?

- How do you think Cain feels when God rejects his sacrifice?

- Why is it sometimes difficult to appreciate what we have? Why do we often want what we can't have?

- How can seeing each and every person as made *b'tzelem Elohim* help us to appreciate our unique blessings and appreciate others?

If I could meet Adam or Eve, I would ask him or her

What Do I Stand For?
Noah and the Flood

Essential Questions: What can we learn from Noah about staying true to our beliefs and values, even when others don't support us? What makes it difficult to stay true to our beliefs, and how can we overcome these difficulties?

Detail of mosaic in
Basilica San Marco, Venice

Get on the Move

Play tug of war. Half of your classmates hold one end of the rope and half hold the other end. When one team loses, one or two people from the losing team go over to the winning team. Then play the game again.

How does it feel to be on the winning team or to move to the winning team?

_____

_____

_____

How does it feel to be on the smaller team, as everyone gradually moves to the other side?

_____

_____

_____

_____

_____

Illustration from the
Nuremberg Chronicle, 1493

Noah and the Flood

In the Bible, we read:

> God saw that the people of earth
> were very wicked, and that everything
> they thought and planned was nothing
> but evil all the time…. But Noah found favor in God's
> eyes…. God said to Noah: "…Make yourself an ark…. I am going
> to bring a flood of waters on the earth to destroy all living creatures from
> under the sky, everything that is on the earth will die. But I will make a
> covenant with you, and you will come into the ark—you, your sons, your
> wife, and your sons' wives with you. And of every living creature, you will
> take two of each into the ark to keep alive with you; they will be male and
> female." (Genesis 6:5–7:23)

Imagine and act out one or more of the following conversations:

1. Noah responds to God after God tells him about the upcoming Flood and building the ark.

2. Noah tells his wife, his three sons, and his daughters-in-law about the Flood and the ark.

3. Noah's neighbors see him building the ark and come to ask what is going on.

4. Noah and his family talk about how life on the ark is hard and how they are coping.

5. After 40 days, when the rain finally stops, Noah and his family talk about their hopes and fears for the future.

Imagine that you are Noah in the skit you acted out. How do you feel about being singled out to survive and start the world anew?

I feel _____

_____

_____

Digging Deeper

Toward the beginning of the story of Noah and the Flood, the Torah tells us that "Noah was a righteous (צַדִּיק—tzaddik) and wholehearted man in his generation." (Genesis 6:9)

What do you think it means for Noah to be "righteous and wholehearted"? Give some examples of things he might have done.

_____

_____

_____

Why do you think the Torah adds the words "in his generation"? Why does it matter how Noah's righteousness compared to the people around him?

_____

_____

_____

The rabbis tell a midrash (מִדְרָשׁ—an interpretation of biblical texts) that Noah took 120 years to build the ark, to give the people the opportunity to change their ways. When people asked him what he was doing, he told them that he was building an ark to save him and his family from the Flood God was bringing. But the people did not believe him, and mocked him. (*Genesis Rabbah* 30:7) What does this midrash tell us about Noah's character and his relationship to the people around him?

_____

_____

_____

If I could meet Noah, I would ask him _____

_____

_____

_____

Noah, engraving by Peter Troschel, 1659

Ometz leiv means "strength of heart" or "courage."
It means choosing to do what you believe is right, even if it's not easy, even when people around you are doing something different.

Do you think Noah demonstrates *ometz leiv*? Why or why not?

_____

_____

_____

Think about a time you demonstrated *ometz leiv* when other people were doing something different.

I did _____

_____

_____

because _____

_____

_____

It was easy/difficult (circle one) to do because _____

_____

_____

It made me feel . . . (check all that apply)

☐ Scared

☐ Proud

☐ Happy

☐ _____

What Would You Do?

You are hanging out with your good friends at someone's house, and they start making fun of Abby, a kid you know from school. They say that she wears weird clothes and she talks funny. One of your friends starts imitating how Abby talks, and all the other kids laugh hysterically. What would you do?

I would _____

_____

_____

because _____

_____

_____

Why is it sometimes difficult to find the courage to do what you believe is right when people around you are doing something different? What can help you do the right thing anyway?

_____

_____

_____

Do you think it was also difficult for Noah to do what was right? What do you think helped him?

_____

_____

_____

Values in Action

The people below, from the Bible and from Jewish history, had the courage to do what they believed was right in the face of opposition. Imagine that you are one of them. Write a journal entry from that person's point of view, describing why you did what you did. If there is time, learn more about that person's story from articles on the Internet or in books.

My name is _____
     (choose from captions below)

Today, I _____

_____

I did this because _____

_____

_____

In 1917, Sarah Schenirer established Bais Ya'akov in Poland, the first network of Jewish schools for girls, at a time when most of Schenirer's contemporaries did not believe in Jewish education for girls.

When the Israelites are about to enter the land of Israel, Moses sends twelve spies ahead to scope out the land. Ten spies bring back negative reports, but Caleb and Joshua stand against them, tell of the land's goodness, and assure the Israelites they will be able to conquer the land. (Numbers 13–14)

Spies Report of Canaan

Values in Action continues on the next page.

Pharaoh's daughter saves baby Moses despite her father's decree that all Israelite baby boys should be killed. (Exodus 2)

Pharaoh's Daughter Finding Baby Moses, Konstantin Flavitsky

In 1972, Rabbi Sally Priesand became the first American woman to be ordained as a rabbi, by Hebrew Union College, the Reform rabbinical seminary.

At a time when the people of Israel were sunk in a low moral state and many turned to idolatry, the prophet Isaiah urged the people to return to God, to the ways of justice and compassion. (See for example, Isaiah 1:17.)

Isaiah Bible card, 1904

Staying True to My Values

What values would you stay true to no matter what anyone around you does or says? Brainstorm a list of values as a class, and then fill in the ones that are most important to you below.

The values that are most important to me are…

☐ Honesty

☐ Family loyalty

☐ Jewish tradition

☐ _____

☐ _____

☐ _____

☐ _____

I chose these values because _____

_____

_____

Try This!

Ask your family members what values they would follow no matter what anyone around them does or says. Present your family's values to your class as a collage, video, PowerPoint, or poster.

Torah Timeline:

What Happens When Everyone Does the Same Thing?

Cain and Abel   **Noah and the Flood**   **Tower of Babel**   **Abraham**

Tower of Babel, Pieter Bruegel the Elder, 1563

After the Flood, the people multiplied and became numerous. The story continues.

Everyone in the world had one language and the same words. When they migrated from the east, they came upon a valley in the land of Shinar and settled there. They said to one another, "… Let us build a city and a tower that reach the sky, and let us make a name for ourselves so that we will not be scattered over the face of the land."

God came down to look at the city and tower that they had built, and said, "Now they are one nation and one language, and they begin to do this! Nothing they plan to do will be out of their reach. Let's go down and confuse their language [by making the people speak different languages] so that they will not understand each other." So God scattered them across the earth from there, and they stopped building the city.
(Genesis 11:1–8)

Talk about It:

- This story is difficult to understand. Why do you think God made the people speak different languages and scattered them across the earth? Was it a punishment? If so, for what?

- The ancient rabbis told a midrash (מִדְרָשׁ—an interpretation of biblical texts) that said that if a person fell and died while building the tower, no one took notice, but if a brick fell, everyone mourned. (*Pirkei De-Rabbi Eliezer* 24) According to this midrash, why might God have been punishing the people?

- What do you think could happen if everyone always does the same thing? What if there isn't someone like Noah to have the courage to do something different?

Where Do I Find Faith and Hope?
Abraham and Sarah

Essential Questions: How can the story of Abraham and Sarah going to Canaan inspire us to have faith to take risks and make changes in our lives? What gives us the strength to try something new, to make our lives or the world better?

Doing Something New

Have you ever moved to a new home or school? Or found the courage to make a big change in your life, even if you didn't know exactly where that change would take you?

One big change that I made was _____

_____

_____

It was easy/difficult (circle one) to do because _____

_____

_____

It made me feel . . . (check all that apply)

- ☐ Proud
- ☐ Excited
- ☐ Nervous
- ☐ Hopeful
- ☐ _____
- ☐ _____
- ☐ _____

Abram and Sarai Go to Canaan

Read the story below describing the journey of Abram and Sarai (later known as Abraham and Sarah) from Haran to Canaan. Then draw arrows on the map to show how they traveled.

God said to Abram, "לֶךְ-לְךָ—Lech lecha—Go forth from your land, from your birthplace, from your family's home, to the land that I will show you. I will make you a great nation, and I will bless you and make your name great, and you will be a blessing...."

So Abram went...with his wife Sarai, and his nephew Lot, and...the people that they had gathered in Haran, and they went to the land of Canaan....

Abram [and Sarai] traveled through the land to Shechem and Elon Moreh....

God appeared to Abram and said, "I will give this land to your descendants." Abram made an altar to God who had appeared to him.

From there, [they] traveled to the hill country east of Bethel, where [Abram] pitched his tent.... [Abram] made an altar to God and called in the name of God. Then Abram [and Sarai] continued traveling toward the Negev. (Genesis 12:1–9)

Abraham's Journey from Ur to Canaan, József Molnár, 1850

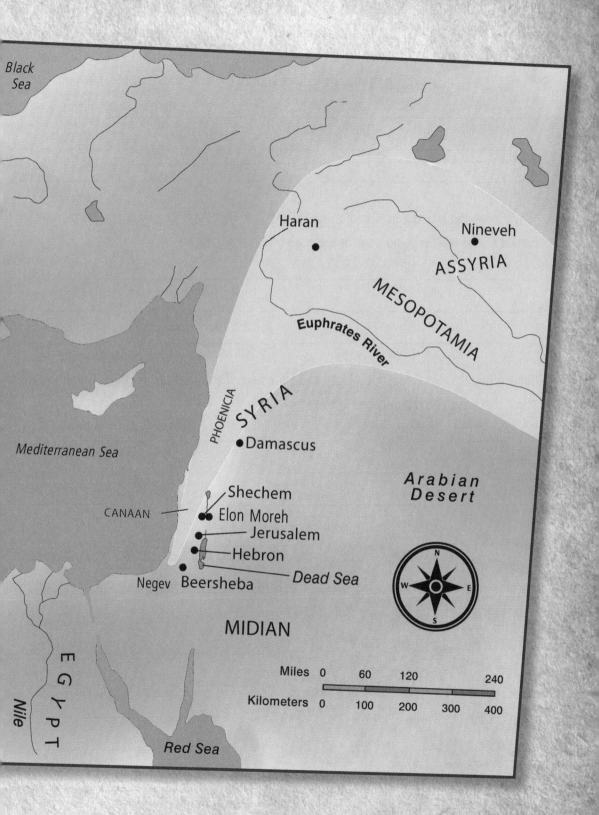

Black
Sea

Haran

Nineveh

ASSYRIA

MESOPOTAMIA

Euphrates River

PHOENICIA

SYRIA

Mediterranean Sea

Damascus

Arabian
Desert

Shechem

CANAAN

Elon Moreh

Jerusalem

Hebron

Dead Sea

Negev   Beersheba

MIDIAN

N
W   E
S

E
G
Y
P
T

Nile

Red Sea

| Miles | 0 | | 60 | 120 | | 240 |
| Kilometers | 0 | 100 | 200 | 300 | 400 |

When the Torah repeats words, phrases, or ideas, it often is calling our attention to something important. Why do you think the text describes the land that Abram and Sarai are leaving in three different ways: "from your land, from your birthplace, from your family's home"?

_____

_____

_____

Why do you think God tells Abram to go to "the land that I will show you" rather than telling him where he will be going and some details about that land?

_____

_____

_____

Some argue that God is testing Abram and Sarai here. If so, what do you think God finds out about them through their actions in this story?

_____

_____

_____

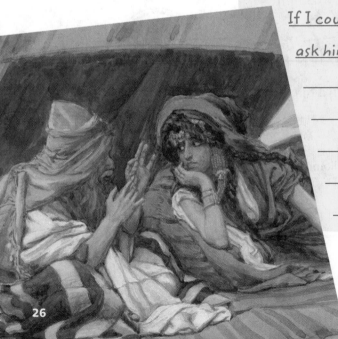

If I could meet Abram or Sarai, I would
ask him or her _____

_____

_____

_____

_____

Abram's Counsel to Sarai, James Jacques Joseph Tissot, 1896–1902

Stepping into Their Sandals

Sometimes the best way to get to know someone is to imagine that you are standing in their shoes. So step into Abram and Sarai's sandals, and picture yourself on the evening before you are to leave your home in Haran to travel to the land of Canaan. Write a series of text messages or emails from Abram or Sarai's point of view describing their feelings on that evening.

I am _____

_____

_____

I feel _____

_____

_____

I am scared about _____

_____

_____

I hope that _____

_____

_____

Bitachon means "trust" or "faith." What were the risks that Abram and Sarai took in going to Canaan? What were the possible consequences?

_____

_____

_____

Bitachon can mean trust in yourself, in God, or in friends and family who help you to do your best. How do Abram and Sarai's *bitachon* and faith in God help them to leave Haran and journey to a new land?

_____

_____

_____

Singing Together

Listen to "L'Chi Lach," a song by Debbie Friedman based on the story of Abram and Sarai. (You can find it on YouTube.) This song is not only about them, but about anyone who is going on a journey.

List different kinds of journeys:

_____   _____

_____   _____

_____   _____

How could singing this song as a group or community give strength to someone going on a journey?

_____

_____

_____

inspire

Try This!

Interview a parent, grandparent, or older relative about someone in your family who took a risk to start something new—whether it was immigrating to the United States, starting an innovative project or organization, or beginning a new job.

Write down the story to share with the class. If possible, bring family photos to illustrate the story. Do you think this person showed *bitachon*? How?

spiritual

Values in Action

Throughout the Bible and Jewish history, Jews have had the *bitachon* to leave behind the familiar and make big changes in their lives and the lives of our people. Imagine you are one of the people in the images below. Who or what did you have trust or faith in?

My name is _____
(choose from captions below)

I have bitachon in _____

_____

_____

_____

The Israelites crossed the Sea of Reeds, leaving behind their lives as slaves in Egypt and starting a journey in the desert that would ultimately take them to the Promised Land of Israel. (Exodus 14)

In 167 BCE, the Maccabees fought the far more powerful Greek army for the right to control their own land and observe their religion.

Judas Maccabeus Before the Army of Nicanor, Gustave Doré

When the Temple in Jerusalem was destroyed in 70 CE, Rabbi Yochanan Ben Zakkai established a new center for the Jewish people in Yavneh, in central Israel. This center helped radically change the focus of Judaism to Torah learning and prayer, instead of giving sacrifices to God.

Destruction of the Second Temple

Tens of thousands of Ethiopian Jews made aliyah (עֲלִיָּה—immigrated to Israel), beginning in the late 1970s. Many of them fled by foot to refugee camps in Sudan, a treacherous journey that took two to four weeks. From Sudan, they were airlifted to Israel.

If I could meet _____
                              (choose from captions above)
I would ask him or her _____

_____

_____

_____

_____

Bitachon and Me

Each day, I have *bitachon* in . . . (check all that apply)

☐ My teacher to help me learn new things

☐ My family to _____

☐ My friends to _____

☐ Myself to _____

☐ _____

☐ _____

☐ _____

One new thing that I would like to have the bitachon to do is _____

_____

_____

_____

My bitachon in _____ will help me do this.

Torah Timeline:
Abraham's Faith in God—It's Complicated

| Abram and Sarai Leave for Canaan | Sodom and Gomorrah | God Commands Abraham to Sacrifice Isaac | Rebekah at the Well |

"Lech lecha..." begins the story of Abraham's relationship with God. This relationship grows and changes throughout Abraham's life, although his *bitachon* in God remains strong. Sometimes Abraham struggles with God, and other times he listens without questioning. The following two stories stand out in the development of Abraham and God's relationship.

In the first story, many years after Abraham settles in Canaan,

> God says to Abraham: "The cry of Sodom and Gomorrah is great, and the people there have committed terrible sins. I will go down to see whether they have acted entirely [as bad as] the cry that has come up to me...." Abraham comes forward and responds, "Will you destroy innocent people along with those who are guilty [by destroying the entire cities of Sodom and Gomorrah]?... Will the judge of the earth not do justly?" (Genesis 18:20–25)

In another key story that readers of the Bible have struggled with for centuries,

> God tells Abraham, "Take your son, your favorite one, Isaac, whom you love, and go to the land of Moriah and offer him there as a burnt offering...." (Genesis 22:2) Abraham prepares to sacrifice Isaac as God has commanded him, but at the last minute the angel of God stops Abraham and tells him to sacrifice an animal instead.

Talk about It:

- Why does Abraham argue with God in the Sodom and Gomorrah story?

- Does arguing mean he has any less *bitachon* in God? Do you think someone can have *bitachon* in God and still struggle with some of the things that God does? Why?

- Abraham's willingness to sacrifice his son is very difficult to understand. What do you think makes Abraham obey God without question in this case?

- In these two stories, as well as in the story on page 24, Abraham's *bitachon* in God shapes the way he lives his life. How does *bitachon* help shape the way you live your life?

How Can I Pay It Forward?
Rebekah at the Well

Essential Questions: How can the story of Rebekah at the well inspire us to act with kindness in our families? How can we do acts of kindness in our everyday lives?

What Would You Look For?

In the first three chapters, we focused on how to be our best selves as individuals. In the next four chapters, we are going to focus on how to be our best selves within our family.

Which *midot* (מִדּוֹת — qualities or character traits) are most important to you in a family member? Choose three.

☐ Responsibility

☐ Honesty

☐ Humor

☐ Good listening

☐ Kindness

☐ Fun

☐ Intelligence

☐ _____

☐ _____

☐ _____

As a class, debate and then vote on which three *midot* you think are the most important.

When Abraham sends his servant Eliezer to find a wife for his son Isaac, Eliezer has to figure out which *midah* to look for in the woman who will become part of the Jewish people's "first family." Which *midah* does he choose and why? Keep this question in mind as you read the story on the next page.

Telling the Story

Rebekah at the Well

Make your own comic strip by illustrating the story below, from Genesis 24.

Abraham said to his servant: "Go to my homeland, my birthplace, and find a wife for my son Isaac." The servant took ten of his master's camels and went out, with all the goods of his master in his hand, to Aram-naharaim, the city of Nahor, Abraham's brother.

Abraham's servant made the camels kneel down by the well. He said: "O God, let it come to pass that when I say to a young woman, 'Please pour water for me from your pitcher, that I may drink,' and the young woman replies, 'Drink, and I will also give your camels water to drink,' let that woman be the one whom You have chosen for Your servant Isaac." Before the servant was done speaking, Rebekah came out with her pitcher on her shoulder.

The servant ran to meet her, and said, "Please give me a little water from your pitcher." She said, "Drink, my lord." And she hurried to let down her pitcher and give him water to drink. When she was done giving him water, she said, "I will also draw water for your camels to drink, until they are done drinking." And she hurried to pour the water from her pitcher into the camel's trough and ran again to the well to draw water for all his camels.

The servant said to her, "Please tell me, whose daughter are you?" She said, "I am the daughter of Bethuel, son of Milcah, the wife of Nahor." The man bowed down to God and said: "Blessed is God, who led me to the house of my master's family."

Digging Deeper

How else could Rebekah have responded when Abraham's servant asked her for water?

Page from the *Vienna Genesis,* sixth century

Rebekah could have... (write down different options)

☐ _____

☐ _____

☐ _____

☐ _____

Why do you think Rebekah chose to respond as she did?

_____

_____

_____

What can we learn about Rebekah from this choice?

_____

_____

_____

Do you think Eliezer came up with a good way to test Rebekah's character? Why or why not?

_____

_____

_____

If I could meet Rebekah, I would ask her _____

_____

_____

_____

Stained glass window, Germany

37

Making Meaning
חֶסֶד

Chesed means "kindness." Do you think it was hard for Rebekah to act with *chesed* toward Eliezer? Why or why not?

_____

_____

_____

Think of a time that someone asked you to do something kind but it was hard to do.

Someone asked me to _____

_____

_____

I decided to do it/not do it (circle one) *because* _____

_____

_____

I was happy/not happy (circle one) *with my decision because* _____

_____

_____

Try This!

Ask your family which *midot* they believe are the most important in a family member. Together, make up a test you would use to see if you would want Rebekah to join your family.

Get on the Move

This game is like Telephone, but instead of whispering something to the person next to you, you make a face. Here's how to play:

- Everyone sits in a circle with their eyes closed. One person is chosen to begin.

- That person taps the person next to them, who opens his or her eyes. The first person makes a face for the second person, expressing some kind of specific emotion.

- The second person repeats the process, tapping the third person in line. Each person tries to make the exact same face as the previous person, and the game continues until everyone has had a turn. At the end, the last person makes a face for the first person.

In this game, an expression is passed from one person to the next. Can you think of a time when someone frowned at you or got angry with you, and as a result you frowned or got angry at someone else? Was there a time when someone smiled at you or did something nice for you, and you smiled or did something nice for someone else? How can being kind affect not only the person to whom you are kind, but also other people?

Chesed Hero

In the Book of Ruth, which we read on the holiday of Shavuot, we meet another biblical woman who is known for her acts of *chesed*.

Ruth's Wise Choice, Bible card, 1907

Two brothers, along with their parents, leave the land of Israel in a time of famine and go to Moab. There, the brothers meet and marry Ruth and Orpah.

About ten years after their father has died, both brothers die, and their mother, Naomi, decides to return to Israel. She begs Ruth and Orpah to stay in Moab, their homeland, where they can start new lives. Orpah agrees, but Ruth insists on going with Naomi, saying, "Wherever you go, I will go; where you stay, I will stay; your people will be my people, and your God will be my God." (Ruth 1:16) When they get to Israel, Ruth goes to the fields to gather food for herself and Naomi. Ruth remarries and becomes the great-grandmother of King David, one of the greatest kings in Jewish history.

If you were Ruth, what would you have done? Why?

_____

_____

_____

How does Ruth show *chesed* to Naomi? What do you think some of her reasons were for doing so?

_____

_____

_____

What can we learn from Ruth's story that we can apply to our lives today?

_____

_____

Everyday Acts of Kindness

Brainstorm small acts of *chesed* that you can do throughout the day, at home and at school, either by yourself or with friends, classmates, or siblings. Make a list.

_____

_____

_____

_____

_____

_____

_____

_____

_____

_____

_____

_____

_____

_____

Choose one of the acts of *chesed* from your list, and do it as many times as possible in the coming week. Share your experience in your next class.

Try This!

"Pay it forward" means that someone does an act of kindness for someone else, and then the person who received the kindness does an act of kindness for a different person, and so on, in a ripple effect.

Run a "Pay It Forward Day" at your school or synagogue, in which students choose small acts of kindness to do at home or at school (such as the acts of *chesed* you listed on page 41). Make "Pay It Forward" cards or bracelets to give to the recipients of the kindness. The person who receives the kindness—and the card or bracelet— then does an act of kindness for a different person, and passes the card or bracelet on to that person, and so on.

Many of the acts of kindness on "Pay It Forward Day" will be spontaneous. If you wish, you can also plan more ambitious *chesed* projects in advance.

At the end of "Pay It Forward Day," fill in the following:

Today, I did these acts of chesed: _____

_____

_____

I noticed _____

_____

_____

I learned _____

_____

_____

What Do I Get in Return?

How do you feel when someone you've been kind to isn't kind to you in return or decides not to "pay it forward"? What do you do?

_____

_____

_____

When is it hard to be kind to someone else? Why?

_____

_____

_____

Have you ever been in a relationship with someone in which you often are not kind to each other (such as with a sibling)? What can you do to change the pattern?

_____

_____

_____

Should I Always Tell the Truth? *Jacob and Esau*

Essential Questions: How does Jacob's decision to lie shape what happens to him, and what can we learn from his experiences? Is it ever okay to lie? If so, when and why?

Two Truths and a Lie

Tell two truths and a lie about yourself, and see if your friends can guess which statements are true and which one is a lie. Then switch roles and see if you can guess which of your friends' statements are true and which ones are lies.

Telling a lie might be fun as part of a game like this. But how does it feel in real life?

When I lie, I feel _____

_____

_____

When someone lies to me, I feel _____

_____

_____

Isaac Blessing Jacob, José de Ribera, 1637

Jacob and Esau's Blessing

Isaac and Rebekah have twin boys, Esau, who was born first, and Jacob.
Before the boys are born, God tells Rebekah: "The elder will serve the younger."
(Genesis 25:23) When the brothers grow up, the Bible tells us: "Esau was a skillful
hunter, a man of the field, and Jacob was a quiet man, who lived in tents.
Isaac loved Esau [because he ate the animals Esau hunted], and Rebekah loved
Jacob." (Genesis 25:27–28)

In one famous story, when Esau came in from the hunt feeling faint, he sold Jacob
his birthright—his rights and advantages as the firstborn son—in exchange for
some lentil soup.

We see their rivalry again in the following story, based on Genesis 27, which you can act out.

Narrator: When Isaac was old, and his eyes were dim, so that he could not see, he
called Esau.

Isaac: I am old, and I do not know when I will die. Now then, take your hunting
gear, your bow and arrows, and hunt an animal for me. Make me the delicious
food that I love, and bring it to me so that I can eat. Then I can give you my
blessing before I die.

Narrator: Now Rebekah had heard what Isaac said to Esau. She called Jacob to her and
told him what to do.

Rebekah: Go to the flock and get me two good young goats, and I will make them into
delicious food for your father, the way he likes. Then bring them to your father
to eat, so that he will bless you before he dies.

Jacob: But my brother Esau is a hairy man, and I am a smooth man. My father might
touch my arm, and he will see I am tricking him, and I will bring a curse upon
myself rather than a blessing.

Narrator: Rebekah then took the best clothes of her older son Esau and put them on Jacob, her younger son. And she put the skins of the young goats on his hands so that he would feel like Esau. Then she gave her son Jacob the tasty food and bread that she had prepared. He went to his father.

Jacob: My father.

Isaac: Who are you, my son?

Jacob: I am Esau, your firstborn, and I have done as you told me.

Isaac: Come closer so I can feel you and know whether you are my son Esau or not. The voice is the voice of Jacob, but the hands are the hands of Esau.

Narrator: Isaac did not recognize Jacob, and he blessed him, saying that all the nations would serve him and that he would be master of his brother. No sooner had Jacob left then his brother Esau came back from the hunt. He too prepared a tasty dish and brought it to his father, asking for his blessing.

Jacob: Who are you?

Esau: I am your son, your firstborn, Esau.

Narrator: Isaac trembled with a very great trembling.

Jacob: Your brother has come and cheated you of your blessing.

Narrator: Esau cried a very great and bitter cry. Esau hated his brother Jacob because of the blessing that his father had given him.

If I could meet Jacob, I would ask him _____

_____

_____

_____

_____

Jacob, detail from the Sistine Chapel, Michelangelo

Digging Deeper

What does it mean to have Isaac's blessing, and why is it so important to Jacob (and Rebekah) to get it?

_____

_____

_____

Pretend Jacob is on trial for unfairly "stealing" Esau's blessing. Decide who will play the prosecutor, the defense lawyer, and the judge. What are the effects of Jacob's lie on himself and the people around him? Is Jacob guilty of a crime?

Summarize the arguments here:

Prosecutor's argument	Defense lawyer's argument

Finally, the judge makes a decision based on the arguments presented:

Guilty/Not Guilty (circle one)   Should Jacob be punished? (circle one)

Do you agree with the judge? Why or why not?

_____

_____

_____

What can we learn from the fact that even the Bible's heroes can make mistakes?

_____

_____

_____

Emet means "truth."

What does *emet* mean to you?

_____

_____

_____

Draw a scene of a world in which people always speak with *emet* and act honestly.

Draw a scene of a world in which we could never rely on others to speak with *emet* and act honestly.

What Would You Do?

Would you tell the truth in each of the situations below? Take a class vote.

Your friend bought a dress to wear for her sister's bat mitzvah. On the evening before the big day she tries it on and asks you if you like it. You think the dress is hideous. What do you say and why?

I would _____

_____

because _____

_____

_____

You really want to play in your team's big soccer game, and your team is counting on you. But you sprained your ankle a couple of weeks ago. Yesterday the doctor told you to rest for another two weeks, but your ankle feels fine. Your coach asks you what the doctor said. What do you say and why?

I would _____

_____

because _____

_____

_____

49

Torah Timeline:
Laban Lies to Jacob

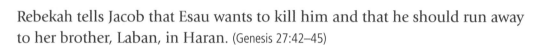

Jacob and
Esau's Blessing

Jacob Flees
Canaan

Jacob Marries
Leah…and Rachel

Joseph and
His Brothers

Rebekah tells Jacob that Esau wants to kill him and that he should run away to her brother, Laban, in Haran. (Genesis 27:42–45)

There Jacob meets Laban's younger daughter, Rachel, and falls in love with her. He promises Laban that he will work for him for seven years in exchange for Rachel's hand in marriage. Laban agrees, and at the end of seven years a great wedding feast is held. But, unbeknownst to Jacob, Laban brings Leah, his older daughter, to Jacob's tent that night instead of Rachel.

When Jacob wakes up in the morning, he realizes that he is married to Leah, and he asks Laban angrily, "Why did you cheat me?" Laban replies that where he lives, people do not give the younger daughter in marriage before the older. But he promises Jacob that he will give Rachel to him as well, if Jacob agrees to work for him for another seven years. Jacob agrees and marries Rachel.

Leah knows that Jacob loves Rachel and not her, and a bitter rivalry develops between the sisters, lasting for the rest of their lives and shaping their children's lives as well. (Genesis 29)

Talk about It:

- How do you think Jacob feels when he discovers that Laban has lied to him?

- What do you think Jacob says to Leah when he finds out that she is not Rachel? How might Leah respond?

- What do you do when someone lies to you? How does it affect your relationship in the future?

Dante's Vision of Rachel and Leah,
Dante Gabriel Rossetti, 1855

Rabbis' Corner

The Midrash (rabbinic interpretation of the Torah) tells us that when Jacob woke up in the morning, he said to Leah:

> "You are a deceiver and the daughter of a deceiver!"
> "Is there a teacher without pupils?" she retorted. "Did not your father call you Esau, and you answered him! So did you too call me and I answered you!" (*Genesis Rabbah* 70:19)

What is Leah saying to Jacob, in your own words?

_____

_____

_____

Do you agree that Laban tricking Jacob was a fair punishment for what Jacob did to Esau?

_____

_____

_____

_____

If I could meet Laban or Leah, I would ask him or her

_____

_____

_____

_____

_____

Jacob with Laban and His Daughters

Choices

Jacob and those close to him make many choices that shape his life and the life of his family. Imagine how the story of Jacob's life might have been different if the main characters had made different choices. Follow the path and fill in the empty boxes by writing what each person could have done instead, and what the possible consequences of that choice might have been.

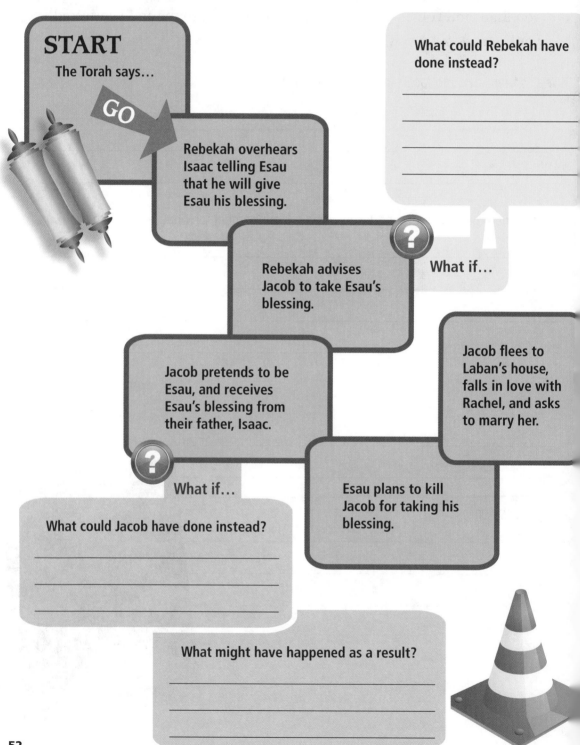

START

The Torah says…

GO

Rebekah overhears Isaac telling Esau that he will give Esau his blessing.

What could Rebekah have done instead?

_____

_____

_____

_____

What if…

Rebekah advises Jacob to take Esau's blessing.

Jacob pretends to be Esau, and receives Esau's blessing from their father, Isaac.

Jacob flees to Laban's house, falls in love with Rachel, and asks to marry her.

Esau plans to kill Jacob for taking his blessing.

What if…

What could Jacob have done instead?

_____

_____

_____

What might have happened as a result?

_____

_____

_____

What might have happened as a result?

_____

_____

_____

_____

What might have happened as a result?

_____

_____

_____

What could Leah have done instead?

_____

_____

_____

What if...

Leah pretends to be Rachel, and is married to Jacob.

Laban tells Jacob he may marry Rachel, but secretly sends him Leah instead.

Jacob loves Rachel more than Leah. He marries her, too.

What if...

What could Laban have done instead?

_____

_____

_____

Jealousy between Rachel and Leah leads to jealousy between their sons, too.

What might have happened as a result?

_____

_____

_____

STOP

FINISH

The story continues in the next chapter....

Emet and Me

It is important to me that my friends tell the truth… (check one)

- ☐ some of the time
- ☐ most of the time
- ☐ all of the time
- ☐ it's not really important to me

because _____

_____

It is important to me to tell the truth… (check one)

- ☐ some of the time
- ☐ most of the time
- ☐ all of the time
- ☐ it's not really important to me

because _____

_____

	As a result…
Give an example of a time when you or your friends told the truth even though it was difficult:	
Give an example of a time when you or your friends did not tell the truth:	

Is it ever okay not to tell the truth? Why or why not? Give examples.

_____

_____

_____

What Can I Do about Feeling Jealous?
Joseph and His Brothers

Essential Questions: What can we learn from the story of Joseph and his brothers about the causes and consequences of jealousy? How can we avoid acting out of jealousy?

Get on the Move

What if half of a group gets to do something fun, while the other half doesn't? Try this: If your birthday is on an even day of the month, get up and play a game of freeze tag. If not, stay in your seat and do a short assignment.

Which group were you in, work or play? _____

How did it feel to work or play while the other group was doing the opposite?

_____

_____

_____

Describe a time when someone else got something that you wanted. How did it make you feel?

_____

_____

_____

_____

_____

_____

Joseph and His Brothers

Jacob's family grew, as he became the father of twelve sons and one daughter by his wives, Leah and Rachel, and their handmaids, Bilhah and Zilpah. Rachel was unable to have a child for many years, until she finally gave birth to Joseph. Then she died giving birth to her second son, Benjamin. Joseph was seventeen at the time of the following events. (from Genesis 37)

Fill in the thought bubbles by writing what each character is thinking and feeling.

Jacob Blesses Joseph and Gives Him the Coat, Owen Jones, 1869

Jacob loved Joseph more than all of his other children and made him a coat of many colors. When his brothers saw that their father loved him more, they hated him.

Joseph Dreaming of Wheat, Owen Jones, 1869

Joseph dreamed a dream and told it to his brothers. "We were binding sheaves of wheat in the field, and my sheaf stood upright, while your sheaves bowed down to it." Joseph dreamed another dream. "The sun and the moon and eleven stars bowed down to me." His father rebuked him. "Will I and your mother and your eleven brothers really bow down to you?"

Joseph's brothers had gone to shepherd their father's flock of sheep at Shechem. Before Joseph came near to them, they said one to another, "The dreamer is coming. Let's go and kill him, and then throw him into one of these pits. We will say an evil beast ate him up. Then we will see what comes of his dreams." But Reuben said, "Shed no blood! Just throw him into the pit." Reuben wanted to save Joseph from his brothers and return him to his father.

Joseph Cast into the Pit, Owen Jones, 1869

Joseph's brothers stripped him of his coat of many colors, and took him and cast him into the pit. When a caravan of Midianite traders came by, they pulled Joseph up out of the pit. They sold him for twenty pieces of silver to the Ishmaelites, who brought him to Egypt as a slave.

Joseph Sold into Slavery, Owen Jones, 1869

Write Your Own Midrash

Watch about half of the first scene of DreamWorks' film, *Joseph: King of Dreams.* (Search YouTube for "Joseph King of Dreams 1.")

A midrash answers questions we might have about the biblical text, sometimes by telling a story that fills in gaps in the text. In this clip, the movie makes its own midrash about the Joseph story to explain why Joseph's brothers hate him so much. Create a midrash, in the form of a short poem or story, imagining what it was like to grow up as one of Joseph's brothers.

_____

_____

_____

_____

_____

_____

_____

If I could meet Joseph, I would ask him _____

_____

_____

_____

_____

_____

Joseph's Dream,
Gaetano Gandolfi, 1790

Whose Fault Is It?

Which actions caused the chain of events that led to Joseph's brothers selling him into slavery? Read aloud the story on pages 56–57 again as a class. Whenever a character does something that you think caused this chain of events, stand up and explain why the character did what he did, and what he could have done differently.

Who do you think was ultimately responsible for this chain of events? (You may choose more than one answer.)

- ☐ Jacob, because _____
- ☐ The brothers, because _____
- ☐ Joseph, because _____
- ☐ Other: _____

Think about the Jewish values we have learned so far. Which of these qualities could have helped the characters in the story to make different choices? How?

Values	Whom would it have helped?	What could he or she have done differently?
B'tzelem Elohim In God's Image		
Ometz Leiv Courage		
Bitachon Trust		
Chesed Kindness		
Emet Truth		

What can we learn from the mistakes that the people make in this story? How can we apply these lessons to our lives?

_____

_____

_____

Kinah means "jealousy." Think about a time when you felt jealous.

I felt jealous when

_____

_____

I wanted to

_____

_____

What I actually did was

_____

_____

Now think about a time when someone else was jealous of you.

What happened was

_____

_____

What I did about it was

_____

_____

Rabbis' Corner

How can we avoid acting out of jealousy?

The rabbis teach, "Who is rich? One who is happy with his lot." (*Pirkei Avot* 4:1)
One way to avoid being jealous is to focus on appreciating what we have. Make your own coat of many colors by drawing different colored stripes below and adding words or pictures in each color to represent what you appreciate in your life.

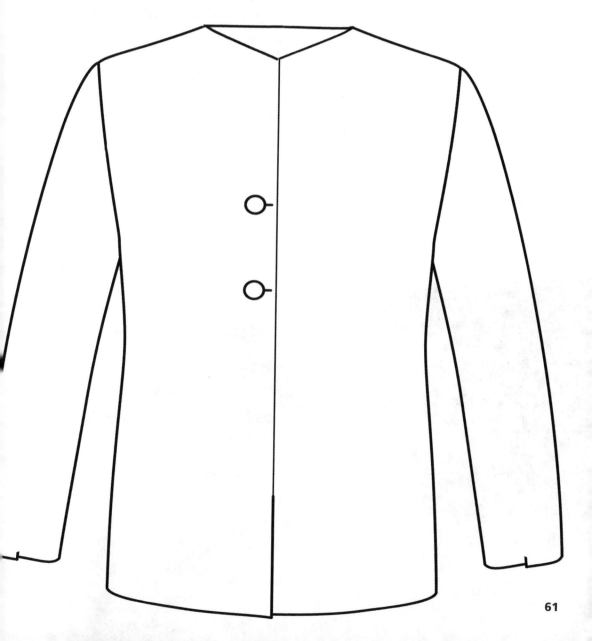

Jealousy in the Family

Sometimes, as in the case of Joseph and his brothers, we get jealous of other people in our family. Even though we would never do what Joseph's brothers did to him, it can still be hard to figure out how to handle these feelings so that we can make peace in our families (known as *sh'lom bayit,* שְׁלוֹם-בַּיִת, literally a peaceful home).

What are some reasons that family members might get jealous of one another?

_____

_____

_____

Talk with your family about different ways you and your family can avoid being jealous or acting out of jealousy. Together, write a list of these ideas:

1. _____

2. _____

3. _____

4. _____

Torah Timeline:

What Happens When Joseph's Dreams Come True?

Joseph's Life in Egypt:

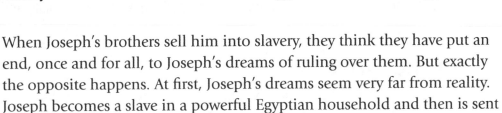

**Joseph Is Sold
into Slavery**

**Interprets
Pharaoh's Dreams**

**Becomes Governor
of Egypt**

**Joseph's Brothers
Come to Egypt**

When Joseph's brothers sell him into slavery, they think they have put an end, once and for all, to Joseph's dreams of ruling over them. But exactly the opposite happens. At first, Joseph's dreams seem very far from reality. Joseph becomes a slave in a powerful Egyptian household and then is sent to prison when he is falsely accused of loving his master's wife.

While Joseph is in prison, Pharaoh has two puzzling dreams. Pharaoh's butler recommends asking Joseph to interpret them, since Joseph had correctly interpreted the butler's dream when he was in prison. Joseph explains that Pharaoh's dreams predict seven years of good harvests followed by seven years of famine, and he advises Pharaoh on how to lead his country through this difficult time to come. Impressed, Pharaoh appoints Joseph as governor of Egypt, second only to Pharaoh himself. Joseph makes sure that food is stored during the years of plenty so that the Egyptians will have enough for the years of famine to come.

Meanwhile, Joseph's father, Jacob, sends his ten sons (not including Benjamin, the youngest) down to Egypt to get food for the family. Joseph's brothers come before him and bow down to him as governor of the land, just as Joseph had long ago dreamed they would. They do not recognize Joseph in all of his finery, and Joseph chooses at first not to tell the brothers who he is. (from Genesis 39–42)

Talk about It:

- What would you have done if you were Joseph and your brothers, who sold you into slavery, came asking for help? Why?

- Why do you think Joseph did not tell his brothers who he was?

- How can you make peace with someone who has acted out of jealousy toward you?

- How can you make peace with someone of whom you're jealous?

CHAPTER

7 How Can I Take Responsibility?
Judah and Benjamin

Essential Questions: What can we learn from the story of Judah and Benjamin about taking responsibility for others? What are the challenges of responsibility and how can we overcome them?

Get on the Move

Find a partner and help him or her put on a blindfold. Lead your partner around the room so that he or she does not run into other people or obstacles, while other pairs of students are doing the same. Then switch places, and let your partner lead you blindfolded around the room.

How did it feel to take responsibility for someone else?

_____

_____

_____

How did it feel when someone else took responsibility for you?

_____

_____

_____

Which did you like better? Why?

_____

_____

_____

_____

_____

_____

The Egyptian Times

Governor Joseph Reunites with His Long-Lost Brothers!

ANCIENT EGYPT—Governor Joseph thought he would never see his family again, until a surprising turn of events reunited them. Due to a long-standing family feud, Joseph's brothers had sold him as a slave many years ago. They did not know his fate—until today.

Joseph's brothers had traveled from Canaan to Egypt to buy food for their family during a famine. Joseph did not reveal his identity to them. Instead, he accused the brothers of being spies, and told them they could only return to Egypt, and get the food they so desperately needed, if they brought their youngest brother, Benjamin.

Joseph's Brothers Find the Silver Goblet in Benjamin's Pack, Alexander Ivanov, 1831–1833

Joseph Plays a Trick

When the brothers returned with Benjamin, Joseph sent them with food back to Canaan. But secretly, Joseph had the manager of his household hide a silver goblet in Benjamin's bag.

The household manager ran after the brothers, shouting, "Is this how you repay my master's kindness? Whoever stole his goblet will become his slave!" The brothers were astounded to find the goblet in Benjamin's bag, and they tore their clothes in mourning.

Judah Steps Forward

Then, in a heroic gesture, Judah told Joseph, "Take me instead of Benjamin! I promised my father back in Canaan that I would watch over Benjamin and keep him out of harm's way. My father would die if anything happened to Benjamin, who is the only remaining son of his favorite wife, Rachel."

Joseph chose this moment to finally reveal himself to his brothers. Joseph and his brothers cried and hugged, and Joseph told them to bring their father and the entire family to Egypt, where he would take care of them and give them food to eat during the long years of famine still to come.

(from Genesis 42–45)

Digging Deeper

Imagine that a news reporter is on the scene at the governor's estate, in an exclusive interview with Joseph and his brothers. Act out the interview, taking turns asking and answering the reporter's questions below. If possible, make a video of your work.

1. "Joseph's brothers: How did you feel when Joseph said that the rest of you could return to Canaan, and he would just take Benjamin? What did you think about doing and why?"

2. "Judah: Of all the brothers, you were the one who stood up and said, 'Take me instead of Benjamin.' Why?"

3. "Judah: How do you think you have changed since the day you and your brothers sold Joseph into slavery?"

4. "Joseph: Why did you choose that moment, when Judah insisted that he become your servant instead of Benjamin, to reveal yourself? Why could you no longer hold yourself back?"

Now add your own questions for the reporter to ask:

_____

_____

_____

_____

_____

_____

Making Meaning
אַחֲרָיוּת

DONATION BOX

Acharayut means "responsibility," or being reliable and trustworthy.

How does Judah demonstrate *acharayut* to others? Why?

_____

_____

Does Joseph also show *acharayut* to others in this story? Why or why not?

_____

_____

How do their actions change the future of their family?

_____

_____

In general, why is *acharayut* to others important? How can it impact our lives?

_____

_____

Try This!

Talk to your family and think of a project that you could do together to take responsibility for someone or something. For instance, you could commit to eating more healthy food and/or exercising together, help out an elderly family member or friend, or do a family tzedakah (צְדָקָה —charity) project. These are just some ideas. Be creative and figure out the best idea for your family.

What Would You Do?

You make plans to go over to your friend's house after school to hang out. But when you get home, you find out that your mom is sick in bed. Your little brother is bored and asks you to play with him. You also notice that he hasn't eaten lunch yet. What do you do?

I would _____

_____

_____

because _____

_____

_____

I feel good/bad (circle one) about my decision because _____

_____

_____

Why is it sometimes difficult to take responsibility? What can help you do the right thing anyway?

_____

_____

_____

Imagine you are one of the people who took responsibility for others in the images below. Discuss:

What motivated you to take responsibility?

What were some of the challenges or dangers you had to overcome?

Miriam watched over her baby brother Moses after their mother hid him in the river to save him from being killed by Pharaoh. When Pharaoh's daughter found the baby, Miriam told her that she knew an Israelite woman (Moses's mother) who could nurse him. (Exodus 2:1–9)

Discovery of Moses, Paul Delaroche, c. 1857

Ruben and Gad Ask for Land,
Arthur Boyd Houghton, c. 1875

When the Israelites were about to enter Canaan, the tribes of Gad and Reuben chose to remain behind and settle on the other side of the Jordan River. But these tribes promised that they would still send their men to be at the front of the Israelite troops fighting in Canaan. (Numbers 32)

Although going to the king without his invitation was punishable by death, Queen Esther approached King Ahasuerus anyway. She invited him to a feast, at which she revealed that she was Jewish and begged him to save her people from the evil Haman. (Esther 5 and 7)

Esther Approaches King Ahasuerus,
Albertus Pictor, fifteenth century

Values in Action continues on the next page.

In 1912, Henrietta Szold, an American Zionist, founded Hadassah, the Women's Zionist Organization of America, which became the largest Jewish organization in the United States. She moved to Palestine to lead Hadassah's efforts there to provide quality health care to all and to rescue thousands of Jewish children from Nazi Europe.

During the Holocaust, Oskar Schindler, a member of the Nazi party, risked his own life to save the lives of 1,200 Jews by giving them jobs in his factory.

Acharayut and Me

I can take responsibility, acharayut, for myself by

I can show acharayut within my family by

I can show acharayut within my community (such as in my school, synagogue, or neighborhood) by

Bringing Torah into My Life

Throughout this course, we have learned about people from the Bible and Jewish history who acted on the Jewish values we have studied. In this project, you will choose one of these people to learn more about, research that person's life, do a creative project about that person's life and values, and share what you learned.

Step #1: Choose a Subject

Whom would you like to research for your project? What questions do you have about him or her? Choose three of the people we learned about in this book, or anyone from Jewish history who demonstrates the values we studied. Fill out the chart below, then choose one of these people to research.

Person's name	What they did	Why they did it (values and motivations)	My questions about this person

I would like to know more about _____

(fill in name)

Step #2: Learn about Your Subject

Fill in your "Big Question" here:

How does _____**'s life reflect the value/s of** _____?

(name)   (Jewish value)

What questions do you need to ask and answer before you can answer your Big Question?

_____

_____

_____

What do you need to do to find this information? (For example, you may want to read certain passages from the Bible, review this journal, search online for more information, go to the synagogue library, or interview other students and adults about their reactions to the person's actions.)

_____

_____

_____

Step #3: Prepare Your Presentation

What have you learned that you want to share in your project?

☐ _____

☐ _____

☐ _____

How do you want to share what you have learned?

☐ Poster   ☐ PowerPoint

☐ Song   ☐ Diary from the person's point of view

☐ Skit   ☐ Video

☐ Other:_____

What do you need to do to create your presentation?

First I will _____

Then _____

Finally _____

Step #4: Present Your Project

Share your presentation with your classmates and/or family members. Afterward, fill out the following:

I am proud of my work on this project because _____

_____

_____

If I were to do this project again, I would _____

_____

_____

The most interesting thing I learned was _____

_____

_____

Here are some new questions that I have: _____

_____

_____

_____